A SIMPLE GUIDE
TO
KEEP THE CUSTOMER
HAPPY AND HEALTHY

Written By: Samuel Rose

Computer Illustrations By: Joyce Rose

ISBN: 0-7596-7319-5

This book is printed on acid free paper.

1stBooks - rev. 08/30/02

FORWARD

If you notice, there is no Ph.d. or any other title involved in the authorship of this book. **WHY?** Because we feel it isn't necessary. Common sense, the ability to see and listen, along with many years of experience as consumers are our credentials.

Between my wife and I, are over 100 years of shopping, and dealing with food providers of all stripes. In addition, we have many friends and relatives with hundreds of years of combined experience. Some who have worked or are presently working for food providers. In fact I have three sons in this category, two of whom worked in food management. One with twenty years of experience, even working as a chef in a major hotel chain.

Therefore, the information found herein is based not on books, but personal experiences of people with many years of shopping, working, and eating at various food providers. Some think if you don't have a big title, what's being said doesn't mean much. Kind of reminds you of big manufacturers, especially auto and electronic companies in America.

They felt only the engineers, and managers, who were mostly college graduates knew what they were talking about. Suffice the thought that anyone should listen to the "lowly" people on the line. After all, what did they know? They only made the stuff. But a very important lessons would soon be learned. The lesson came when the Japanese began overtaking the American in auto and electronics manufacturing. How could this happen?

The Japanese did not believe that only those with titles knew it all. Instead, they would listen to everyone, particularly those with practical experience in putting these things together. The American companies have learned, and are now putting this idea into practice. Although some reluctantly so.

So in the final analysis of the matter, it's the final product that counts. Not necessarily who delivers it. As a result, we hope that all who read this information will benefit.

TABLE OF CONTENTS

For Your Reading Enjoyment

THE CONSUMER'S VIEWPOINT

This publication is for food providers, and consumers. If you are a provider, it is hoped you will put yourself in the consumer's place. As the following points are discussed, imagine yourself on the other side of the counter. Try to view matters from their standpoint. Especially if it shows you in a bad light.

As you notice in the title, there are two words with the letter, **H and H** for **Healthy and Happy.** I imagine you are thinking "What in the world does healthy have to do with serving the customer? we understand keeping happy, but healthy?" **Yes Healthy!**

No doubt you are all aware of recent problems with E-Coli, and other food contamination, which has caused illness, and even deaths. Therefore, the way food is stored and handled by providers in supermarkets, Delis', and fast food restaurants, is important to the health of the consumers.

It is for this reason we have put our book together. Considering these problem areas strictly from the shoppers perspective, which should be even more important than simply attempting to follow certain codes. Codes are only numbers, and words. If not followed, it doesn't mean anything.

THE FOLLOWING POINTS ARE BY DEPARTMENTS, WHICH COULD HELP TO RESOLVES SOME OF THE H & H PROBLEMS.

THE BAKERY

One major problem seen in many bakery departments is **SERVICE**. Sometimes there are too few associates, and they all seem to be in the back somewhere. This difficulty does not make you happy. When in a hurry even less so. I don't know what's so important around the corner. There's always a room around the corner in the back. The point is, they are not out front when you need them.

Often when they do come out, hands are not washed. Those who do, will go to the sink, and run a little water over hands for a few seconds, usually without soap, then dry them with their apron bottom or some old towel lying around.

But wait a minute you say, "Their hands never touch the baked goods, they use either a tissue, or a plastic glove." That might be true, but doesn't do much good if the following happens:

1. Your hands are all over glove before putting it on.
2. You blow on glove to separate opening to put glove on.
3. Other objects are touched such as, door knobs, or garbage container before picking up baked item.
4. Covering mouth when coughing, or sneezing with glove on.
5. Touching body parts, such as eyes, wiping nose, etc.
6. Putting tissue in bag with baked goods when not using gloves. Your bare hand was on other side of tissue.

There are a couple of things which could help to alleviate the hand washing problem. **<u>One way</u>** is to install bathroom doors, so they push out from inside. Then you could push out without using your hands. **<u>The second</u>** would be installing faucets that stay on long enough so you don't have to touch them again. Or they might use levers or pedals like in the O.R. These can be turned on with the knee or foot.

We acknowledge there are a few places that have automatic turn off faucets, and swing out doors. However, most do not. This is very important to customers who also use restrooms while shopping. Particularly if they plan to eat in Deli Centers, now popping up in many supermarkets. **(They'll be taken in at another time.)** The above point is also valid when using those restrooms before eating.

1. When turning off faucet, use paper towel.
2. Throw paper towel away.
3. Get new towel to dry hands, then use this towel to pull open doors.
4. Discard this towel in waste basket immediately.

However, none of the above will be much help if restrooms, are not kept up. I have seen many restrooms with empty soap dispensers, no paper towels, or toilet tissue. Sometimes, towels or tissue might be there, but not in dispenser. I have seen them on the floor, or toilet tanks, on top of waste basket, on dirty sink getting wet, on top of towel dispenser, and so on. Everywhere except where it ought to be. Don't forget out of order, stopped up, overflowing, and unflushed toilets, cigarette butts, and gum in urinals, and if that's not bad enough, stalls without latches, or no door at all.

Earlier we said the provider should view things from consumer's perspective. Remember shoppers, it's a two way street. We too have a responsibility. If something doesn't look right, it is up to us to speak up, let the provider know what's on your mind, even if you think it might hurt his, or her feelings. This way when others complain, they can't say, "we didn't know, you should have said something before." One of the pat answers for complaints, as though they don't have eyes.

As you will note, it is not all the fault of providers. The consumers also bear some guilt. So in this case, the provider can also speak up. Let the customers know how they can do their part besides complaining. For example, it is not the providers fault if people don't flush toilets, or throw butts, and gum in urinals, don't flush same, and spit in sink. Of course, unless their employees contribute to the problem. In this way both sides can help to keep everyone **"H & H."**

Something we must remember is, there are no absolutes. Therefore, no matter how hard we try, there can never be one hundred percent achievement in health protection or customer service. So no one wants to be fanatical, just reasonable in our quest to keep the consumer, and provider, **Healthy and Happy.** The first place to start is for each person to maintain good hygiene practices at home.

 **THE DELI**

Many of the same things mentioned about baked goods also applies to the Deli. However, because of the variety of foods provided, even more care is needed. The making of sandwiches, along with handling and storage of cheese, and meats. Also, hot meals, and a variety of cold salads, makes it essential that good health practices are adhered to.

All workers, should make sure hands are clean, and gloves worn when handling food. Managers should make sure this is done. But even more important, each person should see the need, and not have to be prodded by managers. In fact, each worker could remind each other to follow through on this, remembering the importance of keeping customers health in mind. Don't be afraid to speak up, even though you might take some heat for doing so. The next customer could be one of your friends, or relatives.

The consumer also has a responsibility to speak up if they see something out of order. As we said earlier, we're all involved. That is, from management to worker, to customer, we all have a role to make it work. But keep in mind, it's your money being spent, so you have a right to expect service to keep you **Happy and Healthy.**

Normally, when E-Coli is heard, we think of meat products, like hamburgers, chickens, and the like. Not so today, as recent reports have shown, even fruits, and vegetable can be contaminated. Particularly so, since so much of fruits and vegetables are being imported, where standards of hygiene, and pesticides, are lower.

Because of this, it is very important that all uncooked fruits, and vegetables used in sandwiches, and salads, be thoroughly washed. Do we as consumers check to see if this is done? Or are we embarrassed to ask? After all, people might stare, and think you're some kind of weirdo, or something. But don't forget it's your health.

Looking at the service end of things, keeping the customer happy, suppose this happens: You order a sub with all the fixings, then you may decide to eat it either in the store, or at a home. You open it up, only to find out the order is wrong. Would you do like most people, and say, "it tastes pretty good anyway." Or, "I'm already home, it's too much of a hassle to bother." Try to eat it even though you don't like it, or throw it away.

That should never be the case. You're paying good money, and should expect to get what you pay for. I admit having done the above on occasion myself. So all the more reason to emphasize, speaking up when necessary.

On the other side of the coin, my wife rarely allows a provider to get away with anything. Whether it's food, or anything else. This can sometimes make things a little uneasy at times. You know "rocking the boat" as it were. However, it seems the only way to get anything accomplished. Even though it may take some time, and persistence. Again, I emphasize being reasonable in handling matters.

Concerning the problem with the sub mentioned earlier, had this happened to her, they **(The Deli)** would have known in short order. Directly in person if in the store, or by telephone, after arriving home. I can recall a number of apologies, and offers of a free lunch, breakfast, or the like, over the years. Yes I admit, this has given me greater impetus to speak up.

The sub aside, there are other things deserving your attention. For instance, before you order, do you check the condition on other side of counter…is it clean? What is the appearance of workers? Are uniforms crisp, and clean…or do the aprons look like they've been worn all month? Are utensils such as knives, and spoons used in making sandwiches, and dishing up hot foods, and salads frequently washed with soap, and water, and not simply wiped with a rag or nothing at all? If these items are left out at room temperature with all sorts of residues, it could be a health problem.

It would be nice if all of us could rely on trust. Trusting the food providers to do the right thing. However, as we have seen time, and time again in recent years, that trust has been betrayed. By large, and small providers of food products. Therefore, you have to take matters into your own hands to protect yourself wherever possible, while trying to keep them more honest.

Well so much for the Deli. It is now time to move on to meat, and seafood department. All we say to you, is **Be Careful** …look at the appearance of the products, whether packaged or not. They all say the same about their wares. **Fresh daily, U.S.D.A., choice, prime cuts, etc.** But, here we go again. Can we trust what they say? Is seafood properly iced? How does it smell? If unpackaged, and it doesn't smell right, **DON'T BUY!** no matter what they say. If packaged, do not hesitate to call, and return to the store.

There is no need to feel awkward, or embarrassed. Better safe, than sorry. Not only is your health at stake, but it's also your money. WE certainly would not be unreasonable to make such a request. A request if the provider is concerned about keeping customers **Healthy and Happy.** They would be eager to remedy the problem. Most of better providers will do all they can to right matters.

But one word of caution, be balanced. Even if you're upset, and the provider is dead wrong, please don't make a scene. Yelling, or screaming out loud your complaint in front of all the other customers, will not help matters. You not only embarrass the management, which could cause loss of customers, but your public image is definitely not enhanced.

The diplomatic way is using tact. Yes **tact!** I know it seems out of place in these times, when rudeness is the order of the day. Call him, or her aside, and quietly express your complaint. Believe me, just think how stupid, and tactless you would have looked like in front of everyone. And likely, no matter how valid the complaint, they would do whatever necessary to counter it.

Before we move on, I must relate something I saw today, June 12, 1998, at one of those Deli's we spoke of earlier. The kind that are badly in need of customers. Now I want to make it perfectly clear there was no intent to buy from there. Just by chance while looking for something else, I saw this guy, and what he was doing. He was making sandwiches to put out front. He was not only **using bare hands, but also reaching into each bag of sliced meats, and sampling same.** One for you (sandwich), and one for me. Since I wasn't buying, I felt no need to say anything. **But do you think I should have? Would you have?** Well I'll leave it up to you. P.S. when he saw me staring his way, he had the guilty look. He knew he was wrong.

SALAD AND SOUP BAR

No doubt you like most people like salads. So let's check out one of those open salad bars. Where it starts out looking so nice, and attractive in the morning, then becomes a messy free for all at lunch. But before we get that far, let's back up to preparation time. How is this stuff handled before it comes out front?

We might start out by asking, in what country the ingredients were grown? The lettuce, tomatoes, onions, peppers, broccoli, carrots, mushroom, celery, and much more. Who knows? Perhaps they will tell you if asked, perhaps not. Maybe the ones doing the preparation don't even know. Unlike in the Produce Center where by law, the point of origin is supposed to be displayed. There is no way the customer can tell where all that cut, and mixed up stuff came from. Therefore, as in the case of produce, there is no choice to select. For all we know, the salad mix could be from anywhere in the world. It could be called the multi-cultural salad, or bar. Perhaps, multinational would be better.

Because standards in many countries are far lower than this country, causes concern about health risks by many. What kinds of pesticides were used? Was produce contaminated by animal run off or other poor quality control? Also, are vegetables thoroughly washed during preparation? While not adding to the problem, by using sloppy methods themselves. And since salads are eaten raw, quality control is of the essence. Remember, no matter how well you wash, there are contaminates that still remain. Some can only be removed by cooking, and others that are poisonous, like some pesticides, even cooking won't help.

So if you are a concerned person, what do you do? Should you ask the manager? And if so, would the answer be straight? As said earlier, would he, or she even know? Why do I say this? Many times while shopping, I have seen deli workers go to produce, and pick up various items. They usually had a slip, or receipt book to have someone in produce sign off. But the question is, "where did the produce come from?" Was it Mexico, Ecuador, Peru, Chile, Israel, who knows what they picked up from where?

Do you really believe it even entered their minds about something like that? In all probability the only thing that concerned them was, let's see, we need tomatoes, onions, lettuce, celery, whatever. And back to the deli. So more than likely you will end up with a "I don't know where it came from salad." Or a who cares where it came from salad. We have the stuff, let's make the salad. I might add that the same principle applies to sandwich toppings.

Therefore, the problem facing consumers is, not only where the produce comes from, but once it does, is it made known? and, properly handled. The fact is, there is no stopping the influx of foods from around the world. So we must live with it, but at the same time, educate ourselves about dangers.

As indicated earlier there is no perfect solution. But like medicine, the more we understand, the better we can take care of ourselves.

Now, assume we've gotten past the where it came from, and how it's prepared scenario, what's next? The problem now is us. Yes, us. The provider and consumer. How so? We'll see in a moment.

First, the provider doesn't protect salad bar from the environment. It's always open, no lid of any kind to keep things out. Such as, the friendly fly, or people, including employees, and customers from brushing up against bar as they go about their business. While coughing, and sneezing on the way.

Then there are us on the other side of the counter. The ones trying to keep the providers honest, in keeping us **Healthy and Happy.** Now we are under the microscope. Why? let's take a look. We are so busy keeping an eye on those serving us, we forget to watch ourselves.

Remember the beautiful salad bar, the deli put out in the morning? The one they spray with chemicals so they wouldn't wilt, so you could get your (5) portions of fruits, and veggies each day. We the public have turned this art work into a disaster by lunch time. The worst offenders are college students, then moms and their little "dears," employees, and seniors. I am not hard on seniors, because I'm in that category myself. However, all of us share the blame.

First the students, who because of their college education like to test things. Like salads with fingers, you know check it out right, only, not with your hands, and if it doesn't taste right...put it back. As you well know, students, do not like to shop alone. Thus imagine the poor Salad Bar being sampled, or should we say, assaulted by so many inquiring fingers.

Keep in mind testing goes on whether hands are clean or not, coughed, and sneezed on or not, and anything else you might think of. They somehow feel theirs is the right to take over, to be arrogant, and self assuming as they do in other places as well. After all, without our money, these folks would be in real trouble. If you don't believe us, just look at all the welcome student signs all over town. I guess they have a point, but they're still wrong. Fortunately, not all students are that way.

The next worst offenders are moms with kids. The well behaved kid sitting in a shopping cart. Now some stores have special carts, allowing two well behaved kids to go shopping with mom. But let me back up for a moment. Nowadays, dads also do quite a bit of shopping. Therefore, we might have dad with two well behaved kids at the Salad Bar.

So whether it's mom or dad, the problem is the same, lack of attention. They're so engaged in salad making, the kids have free reign. Reaching, and grabbing anything in sight. You know, the way they do at checkout counter with candy or gum. Only here it's the veggies these little hands are reaching for. While dad, or mom also engage in a little sampling or two. Many times with hands also, perhaps even inviting little Bobby, or Sue to try some too.

Another fact to remember is, while Salad Bar is under assault, everybody uses the same tongs. The ones dropped, who knows how many times, and put back into the bowl. The same that has been grabbed by multitudes of hands for hours. Those sampling hands which picked, scratched, been coughed, or sneezed on, not washed, and who knows what else? Also by now the once salad beauty is gone…with bits and pieces scattered all over the place.

I don't want to discourage people from eating salads. In general, they are good for us. However, we need to keep these things in mind. Hygiene plays a very important role not only in our health, but also our families. Especially when children are involved, since they are far more susceptible to contaminates than adults. So, no need to panic, just use common sense. Particularly when kids are in the family, to make it yourself.

By doing so, you not only select the produce, but also make sure preparation is properly done. This usually takes far more time and care than you are likely to see given for Deli prepared salads. Since your salad is not for sale, there is no need to worry about looking crisp. Thus no chemicals, as in case of many that are for sale to the public.

Hereto, we the consumer must bear some of the responsibility. How so? By being so obsessed with how things look, rather than substance therein. So because we insist our salads look crisp, our produce be as unblemished as possible, the providers feel obliged to satisfy our demands. Now I know that many will say, "I don't care about crisp salads or spotty produce." That is, until it's time to buy, then it's a different story.

You only have to visit your local supermarket Produce Center to see what I mean. Look over the fruits, and vegetables that have been picked over, only the bad looking fruits, and vegetables are left behind. I'm guilty of doing the same thing, and likely most of you are as well.

At one time, some supermarkets tried to do otherwise. No waxed fruit, only fruits, and vegetables grown the natural way. No poisonous pesticides, but the consumer wouldn't by it, or buy it. **Why?** Too many marks, and blemishes, they just didn't look good. So it was back to the old way. Poison, poison, and more poison to make it look good. So why complain? We asked for it!

But alas to the rescue, the new generation of organic growers. Slowly at first, then as public demand increased, there came a flood, in all shapes, forms, and fancy names.

However, were they really and truly organic? Time would tell. As you might expect many were not. They didn't meet the criteria of industry standards.

The only problem is what standards? There was a confusing array of what organic growing really meant. It seemed each grower had their own standard. So who was the consumer to believe? With so many stickers and labels claiming this or that product to be organic.

Finally, supposed strict codes were put in place by agencies to make sure organic means just that. So whether you're working the Salad Bar, the organic or regular Produce Center, it all comes down to this. The providers honesty, and the consumer being watchful, and alert.

UNRULY CARTS

No doubt any shopping person has encountered one of these. What are we talking about? Those unyielding, and unruly carts. You know, the ones that can't be pulled out of the pack when entering the store. No matter how hard you pull, they won't budge. That is until some fifteen year old working in the store comes over to help out. Suddenly out pops the cart. You were already embarrassed trying to pull the stupid cart out in the first place, now more embarrassment by a fifteen year old.

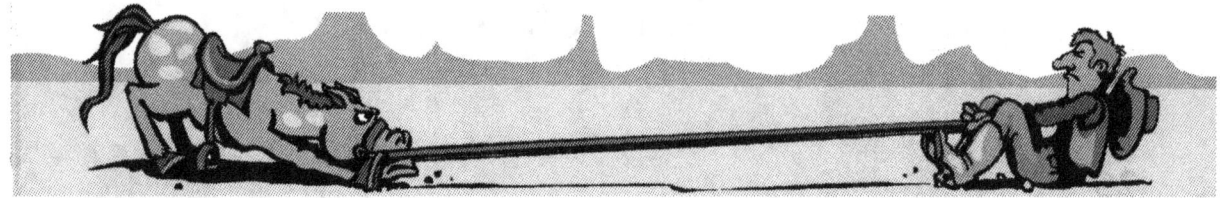

MACHO MAN

Imagine a man trying to pull out that cart, especially Macho Man. There's no way I can let people see I can't pull this cart out. So pull, pull, pull, still no results. Better had he picked another one, but remember, Macho Man. So pull, pull, pull.

Then along comes fifteen year old to the rescue. The problem is, Macho Man doesn't know the secret. Just a flip of the rear basket and out we come. Sorry Macho Man, it's not how strong you are, just knowing what to do.

CARTS WITH THEIR OWN MINDS

How about the cart you just picked out, nice and clean, no garbage to throw out, but with a mind of it's own. Surely you understand what we're talking about? The ones that have a set agenda where they want to go.

No matter how hard you push to the left, it still wants to go to the right. The harder to the left one pulls, the more to the right our friend wants to go. We can't keep battling like this, after all we're supposed to be shopping. So, what to do? Well the only solution is to manhandle that fella, let it know who's boss.

That's exactly what now ensues. The cart wants to go to the right, we pick up the rear, and make it go to left. However, when it's time to go right, how convenient. Yet, the only thing on your mind is, "this stupid cart doesn't want to turn left."

 **BUMPTY BUMP**

Don't we just hate this guy, bumpty bump cart. All set to bring home those groceries, and what happens? We pick out Mr. Bumpty Bump, seems like riding on square wheels. Not to mention all the attention we're getting from fellow shoppers. Embarrassed, we have two choices, either go back and choose another, or keep on bumpty bumping. After all who cares what others think?

SQUEALERS

Who are those fella's the squealers? No, we're not talking about telling someone, but about those carts that call attention to our every move. I would not hesitate to say everyone who has ever gone shopping has gotten a squealer.

Try though we may the squealer just won't quit. On and on it goes, making us feel like every eye in the store is focused on us. Which it's not, but it seems that way. So we try to tip, tilt, lift, and any number of things to quiet Mr. Squealer. He won't quit, so we give up and go our way.

By the way, the next time you go shopping, you might carry a can of oil to calm Mr. Squealer. As for bumpty bump, well watch the wheels for gum, candy, or other objects stuck on. This could be the problem, so remove same, and you're on a smooth journey down the aisles.

That's not your problem you say, that's probably true. But then this is the real world right?

 **GARBAGE COLLECTOR**

There's nothing a shopper likes better than selecting a cart full of garbage. Garbage? How could that be? Well think about it, mom, dad, kids all go shopping. Mom and dad, attack sample stands, thus giving mom, dad, and kids something to eat.

So what's the problem with that? Lots of people do the same thing. However, many people don't use the cart as a garbage dump, leaving behind coffee cups, soda cans, cups, napkins, and other paraphernalia from samples. So if they can do it, so can the rest of us.

Let's face it, if we hadn't seen the stuff left behind, there wouldn't be a second thought. However, when seeing all those things, it suddenly seems to make that cart unclean. Of course that's all in the mind, because none of us knows what has been in the cart we're using. It's just that it hasn't been seen. This problem can easily be solved by selecting one that's all clear.

WHERE OH WHERE DID MY SHOPPING CART GO?

You enter the store, select a good cart, then begin to shop. The cart is parked momentarily while you scoot down another aisle looking for something. Upon returning, the cart is gone. Now where could that cart possibly be? Perhaps one of the following.

A customer decides they need a cart after all, have bought more than planned. So what could be better than a made to order empty cart? Of course they don't figure, you know this might belong to someone. So off they go feeling quite pleased with your cart. It is impossible to track the culprits down since, unlike cars, they don't have identifying tags. This doesn't make you happy of course, because you must tramp all the way back to the front to retrieve another. By then, the only ones left are bumpty bump, and garbage collector.

The same scenario can happen this way. An employee going about their duties notices empty cart, and being helpful, and efficient, returns it to the front. Here again, no thought whether the cart is connected to a person. We can't fault their efficiency, but a little common sense would help. This also helps one to appreciate why women are told not to leave their purses unattended in shopping carts.

I THOUGHT I LEFT MY CART OVER THERE

This scene has certainly occurred with most of us, the lost shopping cart. We begin our shopping then remember something we need three or four aisles over. So the cart is parked along aisle, while we go hunting. The only problem is, once item has been found, we can't remember where the cart was parked. So not wanting to look stupid, (I don't know why looking for our cart, should make us feel stupid). We proceed to casually walk up and down aisles, as though nothing had happened.

By now there are carts all over the place with groceries. After a few minutes we start to panic. Could I be getting early Alzheimer's, especially if we happen to be near the half century mark. At last, there it is, that has to be it. I remember the quart of oil in the basket on top. Now the panic has subsided and we now walk with confidence, just like nothing ever happened.

What I'll never understand is, why can't we push the cart where we need to go? It can't be that hard, can it? Could it be that we're afraid if cart is detoured from present aisle we'll forget why we're there? Maybe so, but then why did we forget the item which caused the problem in the first place?

A FEW SUGGESTIONS

(1) Make up shopping list at home, this will help to keep down detouring. It will also help you on budget by buying only what's on the list, or at least not too far off.

(2) A list is only as good as it's user, so if it's not used correctly, there could still be problems. If store has a food directory on the wall or end of aisle, it can be used to map out where to go. Those that don't, the individual signs hanging in aisles can be used. The point is to map out your strategy according to categories on shopping list. This will save time and needless running all over the place. Unless of course, the exercise will help you stay in shape.

(3) For those who feel they haven't accomplished their mission without at least one detour, **<u>PLEASE</u>** take the cart.

(4) If you must leave cart when first entering store, put something in it. Even if you're not going to buy them. Just grab two or three things at random in order to secure your cart. When you return, items can be replaced, and rest of shopping continued.

(5) When parking a cart which is partly full, be sure to have a prominent marker to help locate it when returning. This could be a food or other item that stands out so it will easily be recognized as yours. Remember all the cars in the parking lot looking like yours. Shopping carts full of groceries can have the same effect. We're so sure we'll recognize ours, until getting back. Now there maybe a half dozen carts strewn around the aisle. So if one doesn't remember for sure what they've already bought, all those carts start looking just alike.

(6)   Never leave valuables in the cart. For you ladies this means your purse, whether you're with cart or not. Concerning parents, never leave your child in an unattended cart.

A while back we talked about what could happen, if you accidentally walked away with another persons cart, especially if a purse was left. So suppose someone did it with your cart, only they're not honest like you are. Rather, than panic or embarrassment, they might keep on going, leaving you with either an empty or no purse at all, by the time it's located.

Parents are all aware of news reports about children being taken, often right under the parents nose so to speak. People are even going into hospitals, and removing infants. A young ladie's baby was recently removed from maternity ward here in Florida, by someone in an official looking uniform.

"That could never happen to us" you say, "only to people we hear about." Well think again. If you want your shopping trip to be a happy one, rather than one ending in tragedy, **PLEASE** watch your children. Losing one's money or purse is one thing, but a child is something you can't earn.

 **THE FRIENDLY AISLES**

Have you ever gone shopping and found many aisles cluttered with boxes of goods being stocked. Probably yes! In some cases completely blocking your path, or the shelves you need. In some stores the stocking is done at night when there is less traffic. Sometimes a group of young people are hired to do only this, and they will be racing around like busy bees emptying those boxes. I wonder if they get paid by the box, or perhaps they're trying to outdo each other. Whatever the case, it's a pain if one is trying to shop.

The providers will counter with, "what do you expect us to do? If we don't stock, the customers complain about empty shelves." No doubt they do have a point. But could they perhaps pick a better time? Yet despite the inconvenience, often a shopper will find the very thing they want, missing.

Often stores are more subtle in their approach to the problem. Regular employees are used throughout the day, thus causing as little disruption as possible. This method is certainly appreciated by shoppers.

Then there are the venders. These are the folks who do their own stocking. The bread, soda pop, chips, and the like. Those trucks that show up all at once like an invasion force in the morning, blocking up the parking lot. Oh by the way, we'll get more on the lot later. I guess balance is the only solution. We can't have our cake and eat it too.

Stop signs and blinking lights are usually seen on the street. But do you think they could sometimes be used in the aisles of supermarkets? On a Saturday afternoon it's like the Indy 500, the busy streets of New York or L.A. With carts piled high and people of every description behind the wheels. It seems like they push those carts the same way they drive their cars.

Sometimes it seems like there should be stop lights at the end of each aisle. Carts going every which way, converging at intersections. Each person trying to decide who's going to the left or right. With lots of apologies, or none. Still it's a great weekend experience, wouldn't you agree? That's why kids like to come along.

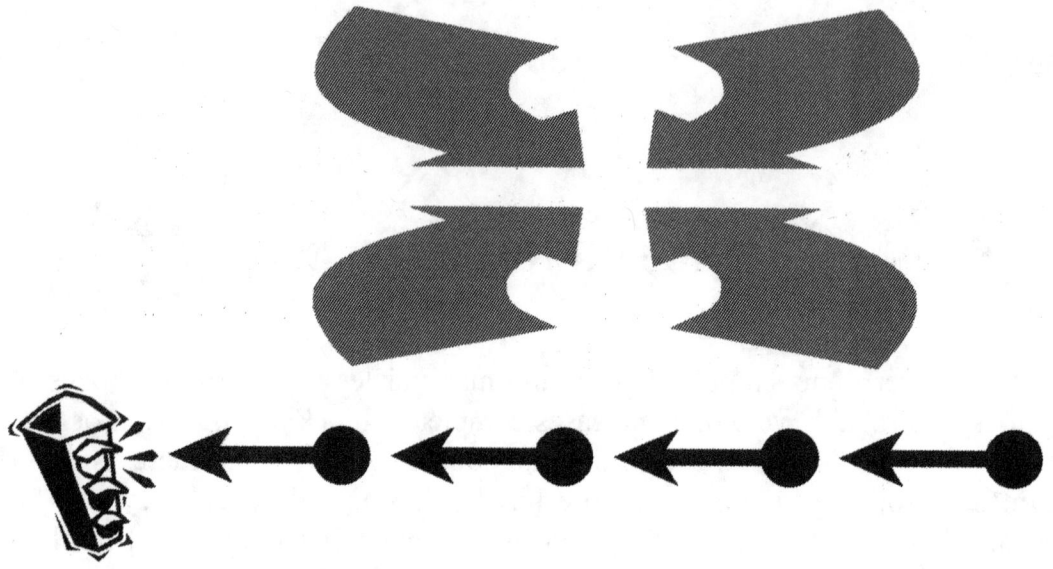

HOW'D YOU GET THERE?

Ever wonder how a can of milk ends up in diaper aisle? Oil in canned vegetables, an empty package stuffed between the bread, or even a full shopping cart left along an aisle? One thing is sure, they didn't get up and walk there. It's not the providers fault. This one rest squarely on our shoulders, the customer.

Most of us have been guilty of some of the above at one time or the other. We pick up an item in aisle #3, then decide by #10, which just happens to be diapers. I don't want it again, so babies say welcome to milk. Would it not be better to return it to the proper place? "Yeah we know, but it takes too much time, and besides they have people who browse the aisles just for this purpose."

Now what about the empty, candy, snack, or cold cut wrapper stuck on the shelf? Do you suppose one of us ate the contents and left the wrappings behind? Why would a person do that? Could it be a matter of paying for it at checkout? Sounds pretty good to me.

AISLE 4 JUICE AISLE 6 DIAPERS AISLE 8 BREAD AISLE 10 OIL

Would we not agree this practice is no different than shoplifting, or stealing? The end result is the same. Someone has used a product without the provider receiving benefit of payment. Perhaps people feel it's not really stealing. After all, they were just munching on those cherries, snacks, and cold cuts, and before they realized, it was all gone. Well in that case why not take empty package with barcode to checkout? Most stores don't mind your munching, as long as you pay. (why would anyone eat unwashed fruit in the first place?)

At this point I would like to make it clear, we are not condemning a little sampling while shopping. No doubt we have, and we've seen others sampling the goods while navigating the aisles. The problem is not paying for use of same. Imagine yourself as the provider. How would you react? Remember in the long run we all end up paying.

I almost forgot to mention the leaving of meat around the store. There are times, where whole pieces of fresh meat, all neatly wrapped can be found in all sorts of places except where it should be. This can be dangerous. Remember E-Coli, and Salmonella?

There are another couple of reasons why a cart full of groceries is left behind, only this time is different. It's not in the aisle or back of store, it's right at checkout. How's that? Groceries are totaled, customer wants groceries, but method of payment is unacceptable. Such as a Travelers Check, low number check, counter or out of town check. I once experienced what could happen when counter check is presented. (For the benefit of readers, a counter check is a temporary one issued by the bank.) Without your name and address printed, usually without number or very low ones.

One morning a young man with baby in arm was ahead of me at checkout. His cart was full with food, baby items, diapers, baby food, etc. However, after everything was totaled, and bagged, he had the misfortune to present a counter check. The cashier said she didn't think they could take it, but checked with service manager anyway. Sure enough, she confirmed the cashier, it couldn't be accepted.

At this juncture, I really felt for the young man. Particularly because of the baby, and all the things in the cart for the little one. The cart was pushed to the side, and the young man, and child walked away. Can you even imagine how he felt. It kind of reminded me of a scene in one of those farm movies.

No doubt this man was not aware his check would not be accepted. But being next in line I could see what happened to shopping cart…nothing! That is until I spoke up, reminding cashier of some contents in cart which were time sensitive, like meat. She then asked Customer Service to take cart away. Here is a good example how one problem can mushroom into another. Who would have thought a check problem could escalate into a possible health hazard?

Another one are those debit and credit cards we thought had a balance, or stubborn magnetic strips which refuse to be read. You know what I mean. The cards that don't pass muster after everything is all packed up. Or ones that refuse to be read, no matter how many slides are made. So not only is food left behind, many embarrassed people as well. These events are not necessarily the providers fault, still it makes some customers unhappy.

CHECKING OUT

Although we have briefly touched on checking out, now comes the real adventures of checking out. The things that make you smile or laugh, and also tick you off. What sort of things? We will explore some of them, which I'm sure you've encountered.

 **FUNNY STUFF**

For example, have you ever taken a good look at the variety of goods people buy? A mix of some of the most incompatible foods ever bought. So let's admit it, hasn't this happened? You probably smiled, or laughed inside, wondering what in the world are they going to do with this stuff? **YUCK!**

However, have you ever thought about the contents of your cart? Perhaps the person behind you might have the same idea about your stuff. Hear them thinking, "I wonder what they're going to do with all that yucky stuff." Sound familiar?

PIGGY BANKERS

The shopper ahead has just gotten everything checked out, and it's now pay up time. Guess how they presented payment to the cashier? By whipping out their piggy collection. No paper, all change, mostly small change at that. All dumped on counter usually from a paper bag. This must be a kid we're talking about right? Not on your life, full adult all the way.

Do you think this customer made the cashier happy, or how about the next in line? No doubt, many of us have experienced something similar while shopping. Did it make you happy? Probably not.

 **TOTAL IT UP**

Buggy filled to the brim. Ready to go home, so let's check out. At least that's the idea. Until they start checking out. "Honey, I was just checking our balance, and we have to scale back." Which means asking for a sub total after every couple of items, until they reach their account balance. There must be a better way to speed things up for those behind.

Another version is having everything totaled, then deciding, we don't have enough money. So now, the decision, what to put back. I hope none of you get caught in this trap.

Imagine having to sort through all those bags, trying to figure out which stuff to put back. Pull out a couple, and total up. A few more and total. Again, and again, until our shopper feels they can handle it. All the while being oblivious to the problem they cause others.

KIDDIES HELPING OUT

Remember the customer who brought along the kids to help with shopping? The little fella in the cart and the bigger one alongside. After a few adventures along the way, they finally reach checkout. The little one starts reaching for everything in sight. Candy, gum, whatever it's little hands could reach. "You can't have that dear." says mom. But to no avail. The more she denies him, the more he yells. Finally, she gives in, but by then the package has already been bitten into.

Meanwhile, the older one is doing gymnastics between the dividing rails and the shopping cart. The next thing you know he's swinging on your leg, and standing on your foot. Again, mom pleads…this time with big brother. "Now dear you mustn't swing on the nice man's leg." He grabs even tighter. "Come on now sweetie" as the little guy looks up and smiles, still on your foot, and hanging on. So what else could you do?…except smile while mom tries to coach him off of your leg.

Does any of the incidents mentioned make shoppers happy? Or how about the cashiers? Probably not, but you haven't seen anything yet. Wait until you experience the Express Lane. The one designed to get those with few items out in a hurry. I'm sure what most of you already know, it's anything but express. But why is that? Well, here are a few examples why this is the case.

EXPRESS LANE
[THE NEW CASHIER]

Why Oh Why…do they put the new cashier on the Express Lane? **I will never understand that!** I once asked my son who cashiered…why they did that. His explanation was "because they learn while handling only a few items at a time." I still wasn't convinced, even though seeing his point.

The fact remains, express should be express, not a lane with someone coaching how things should be done. No not that key! Press this one! The tape doesn't come up, the scanner won't scan, scale won't register, etc. etc. Still being coached all the while. Again, be reminded this is suppose to be express.

Meantime, the line is backing up. People getting impatient, and rightly so. Nevertheless, the coaching goes on. Isn't there someway to train them without interfering with checkout progress. Perhaps having more than one Express Lane, and posting a sign saying trainee on this lane. Thus giving shoppers option which lane to use.

Another possibility might be to have a training room. A room somewhere in the store where cashiers can face all the scenarios often encountered out front. Somewhat like pilots and others in various industries are doing. In this way, the beginner can have a sense of the real thing, without disrupting the normal flow of activity in the real world. No doubt the trainee would greatly appreciate this before being placed on the front line.

I THOUGHT I HAD THE RIGHT AMOUNT

"Excuse me, but other lines are backed up, and I only have a couple over. Is that okay?" "No problem, responds the cashier, I'm free anyway." Now comes the real count while others are now coming on line. "Let's see, um I thought I only had a couple over ten, twelve, thirteen, fourteen, fifteen...twenty...so sorry I didn't realize there was so much." Really, give me a break, a person can't tell the difference between ten, and twenty items?

NO CHECKS

Don't you love people whose memory goes bad after checking out. Whipping out checkbook, cashier reminds, **"No checks on Express Line."** "Oh I'm sorry dear, I forgot, but since we're checked out, I guess there's no choice now." Very convenient, wouldn't you say? Perhaps some of you have done the same thing yourselves. So don't get mad when you're backed up because of this.

 ## MUST HAVE MY CIGS...

Many times people will checkout and then at the last moment, say, **"Give me a pack of this or that."** Why should that be a problem some might say? If you are in line, and in a hurry, you'll understand.

There was a time when cigarettes were kept at checkouts. But because of thefts by public, and cashiers, most stores keep them in Customer Service area. Which means cashier has to leave, go to service counter, get packs, and return to station. Then customer may say, **"That's not the one I want, give me soft pack 150 millimeters."**...or whatever. Don't forget others, maybe you, are still in line.

 **MOLASSES KID**

This particular cashier must have taken a shower in molasses, and forgot to rinse. Either that, or they rinsed in another batch of molasses. It's a wonder they ever got to work on time, or did they?

By the time you reach the checkout, the molasses must be hardening. What makes you say that? Well look at her movements, (we are not picking on her, it could be him too, but usually her) it takes what seems like a minute to pick up each item to scan. Then just as long to place each in bag. Reminds you of movie show in slow motion. Only you wish this movie could be speeded up. Can you imagine someone like that on an Express Lane?

LATE CHECK WRITERS

Many of us have been guilty of this at one time or the other. Waiting until everything has been totaled, and bagged, then we take out checkbook, and without a pen at that. Can you see the smoke coming up from people in line behind. "Do you have a pen I can use…**aw shucks…**it doesn't work." The person behind gladly lends you theirs. Their retirement pen, it's sure to work.

However, the show is not over. "What's today's date?" …"Thank you…let's see what was that amount again? O.K. here it is." "Do you have a Check Card sir?" "No I don't." "Well I'll need to see your Drivers License." "Alright, let me see if I can find it." Suppose he said, "I don't drive.' We won't get into that.

What I will never understand is why people who know they're going to use a check, wait until the last minute. Most of the information could be filled in long before ever reaching checkout. This would help in keeping all concerned in a happy mood, both provider, and consumer.

SNEEZER, COUGHER

I don't know what it is, but they're always waiting for me. Who are they? The sneezer cougher cashier. Somehow no matter how many people are ahead, they always wait for me. Maybe it's written all over {**it's time to sneeze and cough.**} Because that's exactly what happens. As soon as I arrive it's sneeze or cough time. Usually, the wet kind, you know, spray everywhere. At least they attempt to cover their mouth.

The question is, how do they cover up? With their hands no less, which then handles your groceries. What bothers me is why does it always have to be me? No doubt it happens to others as well, perhaps some of you. But what can you do? change lines? Not very practical, and besides how do you know who did the same thing before you got on line? The main problem is psychological, if only it wasn't done in front of you.

UNCOOPERATIVE SLIDERS

Remember earlier we mentioned cards that didn't want to be recognized, no matter how many slides. Perhaps they just didn't want to, **[giving you a hard time]** or maybe because they didn't have a choice. Such as no money in checking account or over the credit limit. Whatever the case, it's a pain for those waiting behind.

Especially if you happen to follow someone with every card in the country. Which they insist on trying, until one works. Believe it or not, sometimes none of them will work. Has this ever happened to you? Or perhaps something like it. How about when it's on the Express Lane. But don't forget, be balanced, be patient, don't lose your temper. You'll probably be aggravated again, and soon.

BUGGY LEAVERS

Don't we all appreciate those folks who don't move their buggies after unloading? Right in front, blocking your way to checkout counter. No matter how you sigh, grunt, give body language, the person still doesn't get the point. Finally, you nudge the cart forward, hoping this will send the right message. But to no avail.

In fact the customer gives a dirty look (like what do you think you're doing?…trying to run me over?) With no effort to correct matter. If most of you are like me, you'll grumble to yourself and take it stride. Just another way, how inconsiderate people are today.

Most likely you're afraid to say anything because of unknown response of retribution. Some eventually get the point and move the cart, or we, the cashier, or the bagger will.

There is one thing to keep in mind the theme is being healthy, and happy. So it's not worth putting either in jeopardy, because of the inconsiderate behavior of others.

OLD TIMERS

Don't say it, I know what you're thinking. He's getting ready to beat up on old people. Not a chance, that's the farthest thing from my mind. I respect old age, because my mother and father were up in age when they died. But not only that, I'll be in that category before too long. However, the things mentioned are just the facts of the matter. No prejudice intended.

Do you realize that some old timers use their longevity to advantage when necessary? Then at other times act completely different. Reminds me of going to work on the subway in New York everyday. It's interesting how their mode of behavior can change so rapidly.

When on the platform waiting for the train, they will invoke all the sympathy they can. That is until the train stops, and the doors open. Suddenly the little old man or lady becomes **"Super Old Timer"...** dashing through the door faster than you can, while giving the elbow at the same time. Who do you think got the seat first? You got it.

Didn't mean to get off track, but just wanted to show what I mean. They use the same tactic many times while shopping. Conveniently forgetting the 10 items or less until it's too late, or breaking out the checkbook when the sign clearly says **NO CHECKS**. Again, let's emphasize, not all are like that. Some are genuinely unable to distinguish the difference.

41

One supermarket where I shop is next to a retirement complex, which is not only humane, but also good for business. They even have some old timers as baggers, and a few even cashier.

Nevertheless, there can still be some problem when these folks checkout. For instance, getting back to the check, no matter which lane it is. Have you ever witnessed one of these persons filling out a check. Not only at the last minute, some take forever to fill it out. I once saw a cashier filling out the check, because the customer didn't know how.

But before leaving this stage, I have to say in all fairness, that some young people don't know how to fill out a check either. And they too wait until the last minute to do so. Some are even college students.

BULK FOOD

Bulk food, the way to give the consumer greater choice at lower prices. Everything from coffee to cookies can be found in stores in bulk. What is **BULK**? Exactly what it says, various foods that are unpackaged in big containers for customers to pick from. And it's exactly that phrase "pick from" that bothers me.

As most of you know these are bins that might have a lid, and sometimes not. Where people can poke, and dig freely, with their hands, (**that who knows where they've been**) picking up and putting back as they choose. Kids can mess around and sample, then throw back in pile. When customers can cough and sneeze all over everything. Is saving a few cents worth the health risk?

| RICE | CEREAL | COFFEE | COOKIES | FLOUR |

The provider is trying to serve the public, so we can't blame them for the action of consumers. Nevertheless, we all need to be aware of the danger to our health these things pose. Perhaps if everyone were as you are, there would not be a problem. However, that is not the case.

 **CHANGE OF THE GUARD**

How many times have you been next to checkout, and guess what? A change of the guard. The next cashier is waiting to take over. Why now? Couldn't they wait just a little longer, until I was through? Don't feel bad it's happened to many of us.

Now it wouldn't be so bad if the change over was quickly done. But many times it seems to take forever. The new person has to enter their code into computer, then the routine of rechecking the money in the drawer, and finally breaking open the change packs. In some stores the change also has to be counted. All the while the cashier is apologizing for taking so long. Meanwhile, three or four people have been checked out in next lane.

 **THE TAPE RAN OUT**

Another pain when next in line is having the tape run out. "Sorry, but I've got to replace the tape." They leave for service desk to get new tape. Upon arriving back, we find out they don't know how to put the tape in. Now one of the managers are called to come over and help out. But even with his help, the tape doesn't want to go along. Remember, you're still waiting to check out, along with others who have come on board since this started.

If they knew what was happening, they probably would have gone to another line. Perhaps the thought was, "what's the big deal, it's only changing tape." Maybe so, but not this tape. It seemed like it and the machine had a falling out. At long last an experienced cashier comes to the rescue, and we're back in business. Just goes to show, managers don't know everything.

TASTY SAMPLES

Just getting off from work, tired, hungry, have to pick up something for dinner. While making the rounds, you notice those trays of free samples. The diced meat, crunchy chips, and crackers and even a veggie tray. Boy what a break, I can soothe those hunger pangs before getting home. But wait, are you sure you want to do that?

No matter how tantalizing they may seem especially since you're starving, are you sure? Particularly the ones that are unattended, or the ones with the dip included. Why not? I do it all the time. Maybe so, but here are a few things to consider before your next munch. Even if hunger pangs are pressing.

Consider the veggie tray with dip. Do you realize that people have their hands all over the place. Picking up the broccoli, then deciding it's carrots they want. So broccoli ends up back on tray. Think how many times this is done by others before you get there, and that's not all. What about the dip, there's only one for all. Do you see what I mean? Dip munch, dip munch. The next person does the same dip munch, etc. Perhaps you have done the same thing too.

There is very little difference with the meat, except they probably have toothpicks. So does that solve the problem? Not really. Some people after first bite will use the same pick to go fishing for the best piece. Picking, and putting down until right choice is made. Don't forget, it's the same toothpick they've had in their mouth.

The same applies to chips, and crackers. Hands are all over, and if there is a dip included, you know the rest. Crunch, and dip, etc. Another problem with these sample trays is, most are left open, no cover or anyone attending. Such as other samples that are always attended by someone, keeping an eye on things. Even here, one should be alert how food is handled. However in the case of the others, shoppers have no idea. What may have gone on before they decided to indulge.

So remember folks, you might be hungry, but perhaps it's wiser to suffer until you get home. When considering unwashed hands, sneezing, and coughing, and all the rest. Would you not agree? I recently saw a tray with all the used toothpicks lying on the same tray next to uneaten samples.

This is an area where we the consumer bears most of the responsibility. The provider didn't munch and dip, crunch and dip, go toothpick fishing, or put their dirty fingers all over everything. Folks it's us, the shopper who's responsible. Although we could suggest the provider handles the samples differently.

 **THE PARKING LOT ILLEGAL PARKERS**

Ever notice the way customers treat the Parking Lot? The place where your pride, and joy is parked. carts are left every which way, except where they should be. In spite of the fact that the provider has politely reminded us with signs where they should go. **PLEASE** put your carts in the corral that is provided for your convenience, throughout the Parking Lot.

But does that do any good? **NO!** People still leave them everywhere. Sometimes there'll be a little cluster of carts in a certain spot, blocking parking spaces of course. It seems like one person will start it off, and the others figure, "well why not me too?" Do you know how aggravating it is to pull into what looks like a parking spot, only to find it full of shopping carts?

Not only is it a pain in the neck, but many dings in our pride and joy, are caused by some careless person disposing of empty cart. Even if your joy is a little beat up, no further insult to injury is called for.

Sometimes watching people, young and old alike handle their carts, can be a little amusing. Take the person who doesn't want to take time to park it in proper place. They look around like a guilty person up to something, then eases the cart up against someone's bumper. Or how about the student who pedals, then hops on, riding cart like a skateboard. Hopefully not running down some unsuspecting shopper.

 **THE NUDGER**

Remember the carts in parking spots. How many times have we seen a driver, not willing to take one minute to get out and move cart or carts. Instead they will gently nudge cart until there's enough room to park. A very risky maneuver, since cart could roll out of control, damaging other cars as well as yours.

YOU CAN TELL BY THE PARKING LOT

Just as we can tell how service minded a store is, by the way it handles its customers, the same applies to the parking lot. Whenever a stores Parking Lot is always full of carts, is a good indicator of their inside service. Most efficient stores have personnel constantly recycling carts from lot to the store. If you ever go to a store that's void of shoppers inside, and few or no carts available, **<u>BEWARE!</u>**

There will probably be poor service at checkout, with few lanes open, and some cases find yourself bagging along with cashier. There is one well known chain I have in mind, which will remain anonymous. They are notorious for this lack of service. Never enough lanes open, no matter how many people are backed up. Very poor bagging service, and parking lot is always full of carts.

Yet the consumer must like them. They keep coming back, and the company keeps building more stores. So if customers are gluttons for poor service, what can I say? Except come back for more. On the other hand, there is a chain of stores that puts the above mentioned to shame. They do have a few problems talked about early on, but over all they are superb.

 **DINGERS**

There is a lot more that could be said about Parking Lot offenders, such as dumping baby diapers, empty chicken boxes, beer bottles, and the like. But there's one last group, I have to speak about before parting company with the lot.

Who are they? The dingers. I'm sure you know who I'm talking about. Just go out and take a look at your car, that's sure to refresh your memory.

What really bothers me about them is their attitude. People will park right next to you, and with no concern about the space between, just let their doors swing open. Many times the kids are allowed to open doors, with no control. If someone gets dinged, well that's the breaks. Especially is this true if party is getting into vehicle to leave. Instead of leaving a note about what happened, they hurry up and get going.

Sometimes the shopping cart can be the culprit, with a human in tow of course. A person will think the cart is stable, then as they get into car, cart starts to move, heading for someone or something. How many people do you think will make an effort to get out and stop the cart? Very few. Maybe because they're embarrassed, or just don't care, I don't know which. The point is that there's a loose cart on the move. Who will get dinged or run over, nobody knows. Certainly not the one who set things in motion. They're long gone.

I once saw an elderly man push his empty cart, which he thought would stop. However, it kept on going, picking up speed, because of the slope of parking lot. It finally stopped when it smashed into the side of a parked car. The man was visibly shaken, he hurried to get into his car **(sound familiar?)** but a couple of bystanders called him to task. They verbally forced him to wait for owner to come out, so he could own up to what happened.

51

We could all sympathize with the old man. He certainly didn't plan to ding anybody's car. The problem here was his lack of care in handling cart. Also his lack of willingness to own up to what happened, by attempting to flee the scene. I often wonder if he'd been a young man, would the bystanders response have been the same? It's quite possible that fear of retribution would have curtailed matters.

Another incident witnessed was a young man sent out to collect carts from lot. He was playing around with cart like a scooter, and it got away from him. It collided with the side of a mini van, making a nice ding.

DING!   DING!   DING!

What did the young man do? leave a note, hurry inside to tell his manager? I think not. He acted as though nothing had happened, picked up his cart, and returned to the store. Perhaps I should have taken him to task for his attitude, but I didn't. Always in a hurry you know. As good excuse as any.

Surely everyone of us have been guilty of one or more of the offenses listed. Therefore it is obvious, that we, the public, and not the providers account for most unhappy shoppers in the parking lot.

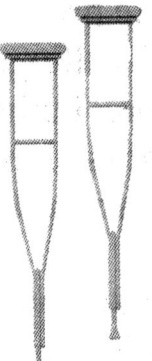

DISABLED?

You will not find a bigger group of unhappy campers, than the disabled, when they can't find a parking spot. This is particularly so when the spots taken are people who are not disabled. Have any of you disabled folks noticed this? Surely you have. Which did not help you enjoy your shopping or cafeteria outing.

There are times when a car will pull into a disabled slot, and a pile of young people will get out, heading for the mall. Now we're not saying there are not young disabled people. But the ones we saw looked and acted like they could be in the Olympics, or at least the Good Will Games.

I'm here to tell you, if those young folks were disabled, then my grandson is, and we can't keep him still for a moment. There have been warnings about this practice and stiff fines, but it keeps on happening.

I THOUGHT THAT WAS A PARKING SPOT

Have any of you ever rode around a parking lot on a busy day? Everyone has, and not a spot to be found. So round and round you go looking for that prize spot. Then at last, look there's a spot. Let's get there before the other guy does. So you speed up, swing into the prize, only to find this skinny motorcycle or even a moped taking up all that space.

This does not make for a happy shopper. Not only is the prized spot not there, but you could have runned down the cycle. This cycle was not supposed to be there. However, we must remember, if the provider doesn't provide a proper place, the cycle rider has no choice. Nevertheless, most will feel all that space shouldn't be taken up by a skinny bike.

I must admit it's happened to me many times, and the response is about what anyone else makes. However, the same thing can happen with those sub compacts, they're hiding in between regular size cars, so it looks empty, that is until you rush to swing in. Surprise, I'm here!

HUH? WHERE OH WHERE DID I PARK MY CAR?

Everyone is sure they know where the car is parked. That is until it's time to find it. Cart full of groceries, conversing with bagger, who now asks, "Where's your car maam?" "Oh it's over here young man," sure of yourself…until you get there, it's "I thought it was this row, ah let's see, I believe it's the other row…yes here it is," …all the time swelling with embarrassment. But remember, you're not alone. Most of us can't find ours either.

If you're a senior perhaps the thought is, "I'm just getting old, so what can you expect?" Well I've got news for you. I have seen college students, teenagers, and people of all ages who have the same problem. "Where's my car?" So don't feel bad old timers, you're not alone.

 **THERE'S MY CAR**

You're one of those sure of yourself. I know my car, I can walk right out, show exactly where it's parked. After all it's a new car, I just bought it last week. Sleek gray sedan, executive class. No problem. That is until you get outside in the parking lot.

All of a sudden, there are six or seven sleek gray sedans. All of the executive class, plus another six or so that look almost executive. The problem is which one is yours? Not wanting to look foolish, you gingerly ease along trying to look for some identifying clue.

But since the car is new, there are no distinct indications. Unless, perhaps some object was left inside that could be recognized. If you're like most, we don't even know our own tag number. Finally, after much frustration, the right executive is found.

Though as bad as that was, how about your key into door of a car that has to be yours, only to find out it's not. How embarrassing, how scary, with so many car thieves now days. The second the key didn't work, it seemed like every eye in the lot was on you, right? I know I've done it myself, and felt like I was a criminal. The reaction is, to get away from there as quickly as possible.

WHERE HAVE ALL THE CARTS GONE?

Everywhere except where they should be. Not in cart corrals, stores or shopping lots, but at bus stops, vacant lots, ditches, and project lots, anywhere but shopping lots.

We have been told by providers that these carts are worth **over one hundred and fifty dollars.** And also, there is a law in some places that say it's a crime to remove carts from the parking lot. Either jail time, or a fine could be imposed.

Does this stop the movement away from shopping centers? No! the move goes on, no matter the law. Yet are these people really criminals, in the true sense? Most would say no. Why? Because they are poor, have no transportation and feel since they bought food there, why shouldn't they be allowed to get their groceries home.

Perhaps you've noticed, that cart corrals are fast disappearing. Why? Perhaps management feels no one is using them anyway. Besides it adds a few extra parking spots, which makes customer happy.

Samuel Rose

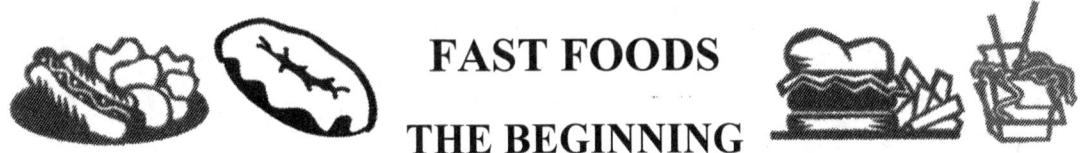

FAST FOODS
THE BEGINNING

Remember a few decades ago in the infancy of fast foods? When symbols like Golden Arches, The Colonel, and the Kings Crown, soon became familiar sights. This spelled the beginning of the end, or the death for local mom and pop luncheonettes. Which in the fifties were popular hangouts for so called **"Bobby Sox"** generation.

Here they could hob knob, and get their favorite hamburgers, cherry coke or sundae. Pretty soon local luncheonettes or candy stores as they were sometimes called, were a thing of the past. No more Soda Jerks working after school. Instead the big boys were moving. Even more symbols and names were added to the list.

At first there was excitement about these new entities then resentment because of what was happening to the old way of life. But eventually reality set in. After all, mom and pop could only hire one or two jerks at most (soda jerks that is.) But now scores of young people could now have a job. How could you argue with that? Even though there was still a spot in your heart for the candy store.

Samuel Rose

CAME AT THE RIGHT TIME

It's notable that these fast food places came on the scene just in time. IN time for what? The radical change in everyday society. The way people lived and worked was no longer the same, and rapidly changing each day. Now no longer was dad the only one going to work in the morning.

Millions of women, including moms, were joining the ranks of the employed. Thus creating a boom in fast food market. With no time to fix breakfast in the morning, these places were made to order.

Opening early, and offering just about anything, a person would want. Most important, it was all ready to go in just a few minutes. In fact, some places were so time conscious, they would give you breakfast free if it took far longer than necessary. There was no question about these places living up to the name, Fast Food. Some would even brag about how many servings they could produce than their competitor.

Eventually, not only would breakfast and lunch be taken care of by these fast growing chains, but even the dinner table was changing. The customary dinner, where everyone sat around enjoying all the food mother worked all day to prepare, was also slipping away. Each member of the family was always in a hurry, everyone with their own agenda for the day. Thus, the old fifties T.V. family was becoming a thing of the past.

To the best of my recollection most people were happy with the change. But not all. There were those in low economic areas, like the mother who didn't quite catch on. After all, when her boys came home, there had to be the usual home cooked meal. None of us complained since we loved her cooking anyway, and besides, at that time we still couldn't afford the fast food route.

One thing needs saying is this. Before the new rage of the big boys coming to town, there were always a couple of places around for years. Remember the little square burger and coffee, real cheap? However, they were no match for the **"New Wave."** Not the right locations, nor the necessary variety. I believe there's at least one still operating in a few places. The burgers are still square, but mostly bread, and the prices are no less cheaper.

THE BURGER BOYS HAVE COMPANY

Just as the mom and pop luncheonettes disappeared, the same was happening to another favorite of many, the Pizza Parlor. Though, as with burger places, a few still remain locally, the main thrust is from the big players. Even locally to survive, one has to become attached to a national brand name. Whether pizza or burger.

Of course, though we refer to them as burger or pizza places, that's really a misnomer. **Why?** Because none supply only their namesake. They couldn't make it doing that. So diversification is the name of the game. Give the customer what they want, beat your competitor by coming up with something different.

It was some of these diversifications that hurt some of the providers. Perhaps in their haste to beat the competitor come up with products, the public just wouldn't buy. As a result, there have been price wars in recent years. Consumers should be happy since they are beneficiaries of this battle.

 **PIZZA MAN**

There is no question that Pizza Man has come a long way from its early days. Just look at your T.V. everyday, there's hardly an hour without Pizza Man ads. In fact some of the ads are quite neat, even better than the product it represents. This might be a little prejudiced from one who doesn't like Pizza. However, most of my family are in love with it.

Not only T.V. ads are common, just look on your door knob, or under your windshield wiper. At least once a week, there'll be one brand or the other. It comes in the mail, in the newspaper inserts, and on radio. There's no way to escape. They offer all kinds of deals, and pizzas of every description. The pizza and burger man are here to stay. At what level though is another story.

For one thing more people are reverting back to home meals, this for a variety of reasons. The monotony of the menu, the hassle, and also health considerations. Not only things like E-Coli, but also large fat content, contributing to cholesterol problems. As a result, some providers are trying to tailor their menus to meet this need.

DECLINING SERVICE

There's every reason to believe the public has noticed a great decline in fast food service. Remember how service conscious they were in the early years. Now it seems like we're all being taken for granted. After all why worry? Our service gets worse, yet they keep on coming.

That may be true for now, but providers beware. The consumers will take only so much and no more. In fact it could be getting to that point sooner than later. Especially with the changing trends, among households. The same way they often reject a new product you try to push, the time will come when they will reject you.

Keep in mind, the only reason for your original success was not being different, but mainly for convenience. Now you're no longer new or different, convenience ranks at the top of the list. So the public doesn't really need fast foods, they use it because it's there.

Therefore if service keeps going in the direction it's headed, brown bags could make a comeback. Remember they still sell them real cheap in supermarkets. It now appears that more people are beginning to bag their lunch or even a breakfast snack. With many companies and offices having facilities to microwave, make coffee, toast and more.

So you fast food guys had better get with it. Lowering your prices won't help if it takes most of your lunchtime to get served, or if one gets to work late because of stacking up in drive through. The question is, why has there been such a decline in service. As indicated earlier, this use to be the prime focus. Hence the expression **"Fast Food."** Fast to make and fast to serve. The answer is not a simple one. There are a number of factors that come into play.

DIVERSIFY

One might ask, what in the world does diversifying have to do with service? Well with a little bit of examination it's easy to see how it can affect quality of service. We'll take a closer look.

It's obvious if it's only a few basic items, it would be easier to store, to find, to prepare, and to serve. The more items, to store, more and different ingredients to prepare and remember. There are more steps involved, slowing down the whole process. In addition with so many options even the customers get confused, not to mention the workers.

The reason those simple menus have become so bloated is because of mean competition. Each group trying to outdo the other, in the war to win the palates of the public. The time was when a person could remember practically the entire menu. Now they have trouble trying to figure out what goes on just one item. So diversify they must, but at the expense of fast service.

FAST FOOD WORKERS

While waiting in line and watching the activities of workers, you would have to agree, they're anything but fast. Remember the molasses kid we mentioned at the supermarket checkout? Well watching these folks it would appear they all took a shower in molasses. Or maybe under this store is a gravitational force several times the norm. That affects only them.

This is no attempt to down grade workers personally. However you would have to agree, that in most cases, they are not the most motivated folks in the world. No doubt many don't want to be there in the first place. The work is not exactly high tech, and neither is the pay. Still many have difficulty in performing even these tasks.

As you probably know, many orders are marked with pictures on computer keys. If any of these should fail there is a disaster. No one, even including some managers seem to be able to use their heads. Whatever happened to thinking ability before everything became computerized/ Whatever you do, **DON'T...I repeat, DON'T** change any segment of your order once those keys have been pressed. Because that register will have a melt down.

I personally have experienced this many times in recent years. Once a group of us stopped at a well known store for lunch. IN ordering, I decided to change one item, which lead to a complete standstill. The poor kid was lost, he stood there dazed, while we tried to explain the remedy step by step, but to no avail. Finally the manager came over, he didn't seem too swift either. Finally, after about ten minutes, we got it right.

Many of the workers are high school students, which helps to explain part of the problem. When we consider how well kids are doing in school nowadays, it's quite understandable why there is a problem. Most want better paying jobs, yet are not learning what it takes to perform, in the one now being held.

 **COLLEGE STUDENTS**

Another segment of the problem of declining service is college students. All but a small fraction don't really need the job, so you can see why they wouldn't be too motivated. It might be surprising to many how large some students bank accounts are. Many come from wealthy families, who deposit thousands of dollars into their accounts. In addition to credit cards, cars, paying the rent, or even buying a condo.

It would also be a surprise to many to learn how college students, don't have a clue about opening a bank account, how to draw money out, or even how to fill out a check, or other various applications. The only reason they work at all, is for partying money. So if the job doesn't suit them it's goodbye. The turnover rate is very high including high school students. Which means trying to train someone else every few days sometimes.

Are we now getting the picture why service is taking a nose dive. Sometimes these young people, even when working will come late, leave early or not show up at all. So what kind of service do you think two, or three people can deliver at the height of breakfast, or lunch time. Yet this is exactly what often happens.

One morning I drove my wife to work, and stopped as we often did at another well known spot. It took fifteen minutes to get an order that should take less than five minutes. The reason? Only three people in the entire staff showed up. An elderly lady who made the biscuits, the manager, and one girl up front. She had to handle the drive through and counter orders by herself, with a little assistance from manager. Despite our long wait, he didn't even apologize, but looked surprised when we complained. This kind of service doesn't make for a happy consumer.

WE CAN'T MAKE UP OUR MINDS

As is generally the case, there's usually more than one side to a story. Up until now, we've beat up on the providers pretty bad, and rightly so. However it's now time for the other side. Which is you and me, the public who bears some of the responsibility.

First we start with those of us that can't make up our mind, when it's time to order. Instead of viewing the menu before getting on line, we wait. Get on line, and then start he-ing, and hawing about what to order. Then if that wasn't bad enough, we ask for their help in deciding. Remember our previous discussion. Those poor folks have enough problems just trying to get your order out. So please don't make it worse.

Besides nine out of ten times most people end up ordering the same thing anyway. So why take up everybody's time by making believe your order will be different. The service is bad enough, without adding to it. Most people will order in cycles, a certain item for a few months, then switch when tired of it. Therefore to speed things up, why not skip searching the menu, order the usual. Then when you're sick of it, try something else for another few months.

Just think how grateful those beleaguered servers will be. Might even send you a thank you card or something.

CHICKEN?   LOBSTER?   SHRIMP?   ROAST PORK?   BAKED FISH

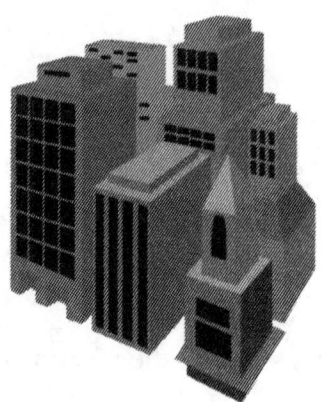

JUST PASSING THROUGH

Fast Food

Ever see people who are just passing through…to who knows where, pile into a fast food place? Of course we have, probably many times. Don't they sometimes get on your nerves, us locals on the way to work or taking lunch?

They all invade the place looking all wrinkled and bruised up from bumping up all night, lying all over each other. You know the sight…because most of us have looked that same way to other locals, somewhere. But that's not what gets on your nerves. It's the fact they've had at least the last fifty or seventy-five miles to decide what to order. Do they? Nooo.

Here are nine or ten people including children, (I hate to say it, but makes it even worse.) All staring up without a clue. And it just so happens, they get in line just before you come in. At this point just turn around, go on to work, and get by with coffee, and a donut. Probably healthier than what you had in mind anyway. Because for at least the next half hour they're in control.

Dad says, "Mom what would you like?" "I don't know dear, why don't you ask grandma, and the kids." "Can I have one of those dad?" "Nooo, I want the other one for me with the movie toy." "Which toy son?" "Aah let me see, I think that one." Can you see the scenario, I need go no further. Let's hope we have a better image when passing through.

 **FAMILY NIGHT OUT**

Just as bad as those who are **"Just Passing Through"** are the family **"Night Outers."** Dad, mom, kids, and maybe even grandma, and grandpa too. The major difference here is these folks are pure locals, born and bred just down the road.

Being locals, they act like the place belongs to them, like the back porch. The kids are mostly obnoxious, of course no one could convince mom, and dad that's the case. None of them seems to know what they want either. Although we can't imagine how many times they've been there. Meantime, while making up their minds, the kids are otherwise engaged. Such as swinging on rails, crawling under tables and much more.

As in the checkout scene, mom and dad seem oblivious to what's going on. Then when they get around to it, we get the same response. "Now dear, you shouldn't be on top of the table, that's not nice, people have to eat on it." "Now, now Susie leave the nice people alone, they're trying to eat." At last all is done, and they're out of there, with everyone's blessing. I suppose none of us have ever had kids like that…right?

Perhaps fast food stores should forget about toys, and all the other doodads, and stick to food. But what about the poor kids? Don't kids eat too? Well you know what we mean, without these mementos, the kids won't want to come. So now the kids are masters of the household? It certainly seems that way.

On the other hand, if chains feel that strongly about movie mementos, and cartoon heroes, here's a suggestion. Feed the kids in food stores, and open separate stores to sell all that other stuff. Think about it, the food only places…would operate more efficiently, and what a boom for other stuff only stores. No special promos necessary. They could sell under their name all year round. Of course, I don't expect anyone to listen.

OFFICE COURIER

We all know what an office courier is. That's the person who tries to tiptoe out of office to get lunch. Then someone gets wind of it, "and could you bring me this too?" So by the time the poor soul reaches the elevator, they're carrying a foot long food list. Consisting of everything imaginable.

All the while, the lunch clock is ticking down, not for the rest of the band, only our couriers. They dash across the street hoping to be waited on soon. But it really doesn't matter, because there's no way on earth those orders can be filled, in the allotted time left. That's okay though, because the boss said they could recoup the time when the stuff was delivered. Do you believe that?

I certainly don't because while the rest are enjoying her labor, the boss has suddenly lost his memory. "Did I say that? Well I'm sorry, you can make it up another day. Right now I really need you." So back to work our courier goes, with barely a few bites. If you believe they'll ever get the time back, then you believe the moon is made of cheese.

Not only is our courier a loser, but can you imagine the confusion trying to match up all those orders. I would guess that a number of them were right. However, it serves them right for treating their courier so shabbily. Maybe the boss' order was the worst.

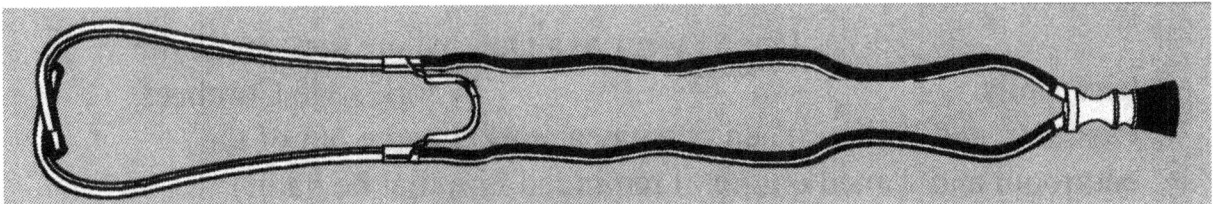

HEALTH CONCERNS

Recent news reports have raised concerns about how food is handled, prepared, and served. As well as the condition of the location itself, particularly in areas out of view of the public.

One thing I've always worried about is, having workers handle money, and food, at the same time. For example, there are many sandwich shops where a person will make your sandwich, take the money, then proceed to make another. So most likely your sandwich was made after handling someone else's money. I believe we'll all agree, about some of the places money has been. Yet, this is done in many places.

But wait a minute, suppose they're wearing gloves when making your sandwich. Well it sounds good, but doesn't help much if money is accepted with gloves on. Then same gloves are used to make next sandwich, as well as being used for many other things besides preparing food.

Once I went to a Deli, where they made the best sandwiches in town. No kidding. New York style Corn beef, Pastrami, and Knish. Then one day a worker came out of the bathroom and waited on me. I reminded him that he hadn't washed his hands. He apologized, and proceeded to wash his hands in the sink.

Even though I took the sandwich then, it made me wonder about past times. Did others perhaps not wash up before serving?

It makes one wonder about eating out. How well do they practice hygiene here or there? We can't necessarily go by outward appearances either. Although this could be a factor. Because no matter how fancy everything might look, if people don't follow safe practices, we're all at risk.

Oh by the way remember the guy who apologized for not washing his hands? He didn't sound real concerned, kind of, I guess you've got a point. Not "I'm so sorry I didn't wash my hands, I know that's so important." He also looked kind of sloppy too, but those sandwiches were sure real good.

WATCHING THE PROVIDERS

Today many people are conscious of their health, such as what they eat, exercise and the like. However, none of this is worth a nickel if we don't watch the providers of food.

All of the exercise, running, vitamins, vegetables and other foods, won't do any good, if we're eating contaminated food. Here is where the provider bears much the responsibility.

Do not take it for granted that everything is being done right. Because it isn't, just take a good look. You will without a doubt see many things wrong. Not only with the preparing and handling of what you eat. So it's up to us the consumer to speak up, otherwise things will roll along as usual.

After all, it's your money, and even more importantly your stomach and health. So pay attention, to remain a **happy and healthy** consumer.

Samuel Rose

 **RESTAURANT**

The place where you take your wife, or go out with friends. Why? To enjoy good company, food, and service, we hope. Although not necessarily in that order. Much will depend on those providing the food and service. No doubt, many have found a lot to be desired in both categories.

Samuel Rose

 **FRIENDLY ADVICE**

Have friends urged you to eat at a certain place extolling the great service and good food? Somehow when you get there, it's like the old fishing story. Everybody told you how many fish they caught, that is until you get there.

In this case, you can't see how they could have given such praise. Maybe they were wearing rose colored glasses or something. because as far as you can tell, the service stinks, and so does the food. Only there's no heart to tell them, and you hope they never ask.

 **HEALTH FACTS**

Many of the same suggestions mentioned earlier applies here as well. What is the condition of rest rooms? As we well know, they can tell us a lot. If providers take time to have clean and nice smelling rest rooms, this says they care. Especially since this is a very difficult place to keep up.

This is usually a good indicator that care is also taken in handling, and preparation of food they serve. Of course there are always exceptions, but generally this is the case.

CLEAN KITCHEN

Most of us rarely get a look at the kitchens providing our meals. Maybe we should. If we did, we might never eat there again. However, insight from those who work behind those closed doors can tell what we need to know.

In many kitchens behind closed doors, the sight is not pretty. Particularly in those 24 hour operations. Where there is very little opportunity for shutdown, in order to clean.

The public in general rarely knows anything about this, unless they know someone working in these places. Or an occasional health report in your local newspaper citing certain restaurants for violations. Which is only a fraction of places they inspect. Many people don't even know these reports exist, or if they do, they don't care. How do we know? Because they keep right on coming.

BUFFET MENU

Just the right place, particularly if you have kids with growing appetites. All you can eat, the buffet meal, and the price is right. But Beware! The same thing that applied to open salad bar goes even more. I must confess that I've eaten at such places. All the while wondering about how fast is the turnover? Is the temperature kept at right level? etc…

Not to mention how the food has been messed over before I got there. So many people handling utensils, coughing etc…over food. Yet they grow in popularity.

So what's the answer? There is no absolute answer. Only the use of good judgment. If you go to a buffet, you and maybe one or two others, are the only ones there, red flag! If the food has started drying out on top, it's time to leave.

LEFTOVERS

Ever leave a restaurant and wonder what happens to the leftovers? Things like bread, biscuits or rolls left behind. Some people I know try to make sure no one else gets theirs by demolishing them.

Some may say it's a waste of food, but remember your health is involved. How do you know who's coughed over them, or handled them without washed hands etc. So to each his or her own. There have been rumors that certain places even recycle leftover food on plates.

Left over meat/rolls   Leftover Bread   Leftover Veggies   Leftovers?

WAITERS/WAITRESSES

It's nice to receive good service when we go out to eat. Those other than the cooks who are mainly responsible, are your waiter, or waitress.

DISAPPEARING ACT

Remember the waiter/waitress who was so nice when you sat down? "My name is Harry/Joann, I'll be taking care of you tonight. Everyone feels so good, smiles all around, including our server. **"WHAT A GREAT EVENING THIS IS GOING TO BE!"**

"Are you ready to order?" "No, not quite yet." "Take your time, as long as you like." "Meantime can I get you something to drink?" "Drinks all around," and finally everyone orders.

Finally after munching on rolls, and what seems like forever, while people seated after you have been served. "Your order is ready." But then after being served, a funny thing happens. Our waiter/waitress disappears. We don't know where, we can't find him or her anywhere.

So if there is a problem with the food or some extra service needed, they aren't around. In fact, sometimes we have to hail down another person to ask for help. Which they don't appreciate, and will point out who should be taking care of your needs.

LEAVE US ALONE

Let's repeat the previous scenario up to the point of disappearing server. Only this time, it's very different. Our server won't go away, at least long enough to let us enjoy our food. We've gone from one extreme to the other from the disappearer, to the I won't leave.

Before the fork or spoon is lifted to your mouth, come the words…" Is everything okay?" **YES** everything's okay."

Five minutes later the same question, followed by the same answer…**YES**. Next "can we refill your water?" …even though it's still full. Before flavor of the steak can be fully appreciated, guess what? You're right… **"IS EVERYTHING OKAY?"**

This goes on the entire time you're there. Until at last it's time to leave. So the question is…Which is worse? The disappearer? or The I won't leave you aloner?

Not to be forgotten are the efficient ones who try to remove your plate if you pause to take a deep breath.

I have had people tell me they don't like either extremes. However, if they had their **"rathers"** they would take the disappearer.

Why? at least they can enjoy the conversation and eat in peace. Besides trying to be too efficient, can have the opposite effect on your trip.

We have now come to the end or our journey for this time. There is much more that can be said on the subject.

As I have mentioned earlier in our discussion, we can't expect perfection in quest to be Happy and Healthy in the food world. However, by using care and common sense, we can go a long way in that direction. **Keeping ourselves Happy and Healthy while enjoying ourselves.**

ABOUT THE AUTHOR

If you notice, there is no Ph.D. or any other title involved in the authorship of this book. WHY? Because we feel it isn't necessary. Common sense, the ability to see and listen, along with many years of experience as consumers are our credentials.

Between my wife and I, are over 100 years of shopping, and dealing with food providers of all stripes. In addition, we have many friends and relatives with hundreds of years of combined experience. Some who have worked or are presently working for food providers. In fact I have three sons in this category, two of whom worked in food management. One with twenty years of experience, even working as a chef in a major hotel chain.

Therefore, the information found herein is based not on books, but personal experiences of people with many years of shopping, working, and eating at various food providers. Some think if you don't have a big title, what's being said doesn't mean much. Kind of reminds you of big manufacturers, especially auto and electronic companies in America.

They felt only the engineers, and managers, who were mostly college graduates knew what they were talking about. Suffice the thought that anyone should listen to the "lowly" people on the line. After all, what did they know? They only made the stuff. But a very important lessons would soon be learned. The lesson came when the Japanese began overtaking the American in auto and electronics manufacturing. How could this happen?

The Japanese did not believe that only those with titles knew it all. Instead, they would listen to everyone, particularly those with practical experience in putting these things together. The American companies have learned, and are now putting this idea into practice. Although some reluctantly so.

So in the final analysis of the matter, it's the final product that counts. Not necessarily who delivers it. As a result, we hope that all who read this information will benefit.

www.ingramcontent.com/pod-product-compliance
Lightning Source LLC
Chambersburg PA
CBHW080420290526
45791CB00008BA/2348

* 9 7 8 0 7 5 9 6 7 3 1 9 9 *